MY WANDERING BOY

Julie Marie Myatt

BROADWAY PLAY PUBLISHING INC
New York
www.broadwayplaypub.com
info@broadwayplaypub.com

MY WANDERING BOY
© Copyright 2019 Julie Marie Myatt

Cover photo: Julie Marie Myatt

First edition: July 2019
I S B N: 978-0-88145-816-9

Book design: Marie Donovan
Page make-up: Adobe InDesign
Typeface: Palatino

MY WANDERING BOY had its world premiere at South Coast Repertory, running from 30 March–6 May 2007. The cast and creative contributors were:

JOHN	Brent Hinkley
LIZA BOUDIN	Elizabeth Ruscio
WESLEY BOUDIN	Richard Doyle
DETECTIVE HOWARD	Charlie Robinson
SALLY WRIGHT	Purva Bedi
ROOSTER FORBES	John Cabrera
MIRANDA STEVENS	Veralyn Jones
DOG	Guinness Prendergast
Director	Bill Rauch
Set designer	Christopher Acebo
Costume designer	Shigeru Yaji
Lighting designer	Lonnie Rafael Alcaraz
Sound designer	Paul James Prendergast
Video coordinator	Austin Switser
Dramaturg	Megan Monnighan
Video & slide images	Julie Marie Myatt

CHARACTERS & SETTING

JOHN, *homeless. Anywhere from 35–65 years old.*
LIZA BOUDIN, *Emmett's mother. Late 50s, early 60s.*
WESLEY BOUDIN, *Emmett's father. Late 50s, early 60s.*
DETECTIVE HOWARD, *private investigator. Early 60s.*
SALLY WRIGHT, *late 20s.*
ROOSTER FORBES, *late 20s, early 30s.*
MIRANDA STEVENS, *early 40s.*

A dog. Big. Old. Professionally trained at RADA.

Time: present

Place: America

Slides and video should not look like they are shot by a professional. They should look just as amateur and voyeuristic as they are.

Scenes should simply move one into another. Overlapping (no black-outs). Like a ride. Uncertain of what comes next… Like a highway.

NOTE ON MUSIC

For performance of copyrighted songs, arrangements
or recordings referenced in this play, permission
of the copyright owner(s) must be obtained. Other
songs, arrangements or recordings may be substituted
provided permission from the copyright owner(s) of
such songs, arrangements or recordings is obtained
or songs, arrangements or recordings in the public
domain may be substituted.

"Do not go where the path may lead, go instead where there is no path and leave a trail."
Ralph Waldo Emerson

ACT ONE

(Music)

Scene 1

(Lights up on a single pair of worn men's boots, alone on stage.)

(JOHN enters, finds the boots, slips them on, and walks off stage.)

Scene 2

(LIZA BOUDIN crosses the stage, carrying a large framed grade school picture of Emmett Boudin at 7 years-old.)

LIZA: He's beautiful.

(WESLEY BOUDIN follows with a baseball bat, a football, and a skate board. They keep walking.)

WESLEY: He's strong.

LIZA: He's just so beautiful. Everyone agrees. I used to get stopped on the street. "Oh, will you look at him…"

WESLEY: A terrific athlete.

LIZA: He's perfect.

WESLEY: That's my son.

Scene 3

(JOHN *sits slumped in a chair, humbled by* HOWARD.)

JOHN: I told you, I found them.

HOWARD: Where?

JOHN: I told you—

HOWARD: Tell me again. But try being specific.

JOHN: In a field. On the grass. Upturned. At a ninety degree angle. Lonely.

HOWARD: Go on.

JOHN: Like someone just stepped right out of them, and kept on walking—

HOWARD: Nothing else?

JOHN: Nope.

HOWARD: All by themselves.

JOHN: Yes.

HOWARD: You're sure?

JOHN: Actually, they were with a pair of high heels. Dancing, jitter-bugging. Or was it square dancing with a pair of clogs, doing some real high kicks in the air—

HOWARD: Don't be smart.

JOHN: I'm being specific.

(*Silence*)

HOWARD: Nothing beside them, a bag, a wallet—

JOHN: No.

HOWARD: You saw these boots sitting there, alone, and you decide you can take them.

JOHN: They fit.

HOWARD: What if they belong to someone else?

JOHN: Why are they sitting there?
(Silence)
Can I go?

HOWARD: Why're you so anxious? You have a date?

JOHN: It's possible. I have my charms.

(HOWARD shows JOHN a picture.)

HOWARD: Have you seen this man?

(JOHN takes a good hard look.)

JOHN: No.

HOWARD: Are you sure?

JOHN: Yes.

HOWARD: How do you know?

JOHN: He's not familiar.

HOWARD: His shoes are familiar.

JOHN: These are his shoes?

HOWARD: Maybe.

JOHN: That kid?

HOWARD: Maybe.

JOHN: Well. He didn't want them anymore.

HOWARD: We'll see.

JOHN: And he walks on the outside of his feet.

HOWARD: Is that so?

JOHN: Yeah. Look.
(He points to the worn edges.)
That tells you something.

HOWARD: Does it.

JOHN: Sure.

HOWARD: What does it tell you?

JOHN: He's bowlegged.

HOWARD: Uh huh.

JOHN: Anxious.

HOWARD: Really?

JOHN: Maybe a little unsure of himself.

HOWARD: What, you're the expert now?

JOHN: Walk a mile in another man's moccasins, you learn some things.
(He studies HOWARD's *shoes.)*
You drag your feet there.

HOWARD: No I don't.

JOHN: At the heels.

HOWARD: Stop looking at my shoes.

JOHN: You angry about something?

HOWARD: No—

JOHN: A little lazy?

HOWARD: Which one of us has a job?

(Silence)

JOHN: Aren't you high and mighty. Mr Working Man.

HOWARD: Yeah.

JOHN: Can I go?

HOWARD: Where can I find you, if I need to?

JOHN: Call my secretary.

HOWARD: Don't be smart—

JOHN: I'm around.

HOWARD: Around where, specifically?

JOHN: You got a thing for "specifics", huh?

HOWARD: Yeah.

JOHN: I own a condo under the pier.

HOWARD: I need the shoes.

JOHN: What shoes?

HOWARD: The boots.

JOHN: Why?

HOWARD: Take them off—

JOHN: No… Man, c'mon.

HOWARD: Take them off.

JOHN: Why?

HOWARD: They're evidence.

JOHN: Of what?

HOWARD: Take them off—

JOHN: They're comfortable. Look how perfect they fit me.

HOWARD: Take them off.

JOHN: What's that kid gonna do with them now?

HOWARD: Take them off.

JOHN: What the hell am I gonna wear?

(HOWARD *hands* JOHN *a pair of flip-flops.*)

(JOHN *sighs, and reluctantly takes off the boots and puts on the flip-flops.*)

(*He flip-flops his way off stage.*)

(HOWARD *picks up the boots. Looks at the soles, and walks off stage in the opposite direction.*)

(*Slide: Stretch of highway. Yard figurines. South Dakota. Texas, you name it.*)

(*The sound of a man whistling, O S, fades to:*)

Scene 4

SALLY: I first saw him in the post office. Standing there.
Waiting in line in front of me. He was quietly reading
a letter to someone before he mailed it. And bored,
standing a foot behind him, I began to pass the time,
(as I often do), with some mental notes: Tall guy. Bony
back. Tan skin. Dirty feet. Old sandals. Baggy pants,
(where I guessed he was once heavier.) Blank white
T-shirt that needed washing. Slight case of B O. Not
horrible, but present. He didn't notice me because he
was still carefully reading his letter, making corrections
as fast as he could...scratching things out, shaking his
head, rewriting... His hair was brown but bleached
out by the sun...in need of a haircut...I saw a silver
chain around his neck, but I couldn't tell what was on
the end because it was hidden in his shirt...I guessed
a cross first, obviously, then I guessed maybe a St.
Christopher medal, then I guessed a locket and cracked
myself up, thinking about this tall thin guy wearing
a locket with his mother or girlfriend's picture in it,
some old-fashioned black and white picture, and then
I thought, well that would be kind of sweet, actually,
and sad, but funny...and then I wondered who was he
so worried about sending this letter to, the girl in the
locket? ...So I tried to read the letter but couldn't really
see much, his handwriting was too messy and small...
but I could occasionally make out something like,
"I'm"..."going"... "believe"...since I couldn't really
make out the content of the letter, and the post office
line wasn't moving, some lady was mailing her entire
life to Japan...I started watching his hands writing the
words...perfect hands...brown, weathered friends...
moving across the paper, nervously brushing back his
hair... And then I couldn't stop watching them...such
beautiful hands...wild birds...tapping his forehead,
(hello there) thinking... (who are you?) ...tapping the

counter in front of him, (tell me your story) smoothing out his jeans, (hello?) ...holding the pen, (write those words to me) ...bringing the pen to his mouth... (I'm listening) ...look at that perfect mouth... (I'm listening) ...those perfect hands... (I'm listening very carefully).

Scene 5

(Music)

(Night. Outside)

(ROOSTER FORBES braces himself against the weather, trying to talk on his cell phone. He wears a National Park Ranger uniform, has a dog on a leash. [He is crossing the stage as he speaks].)

ROOSTER: Hello this is Rooster Forbes. Uh... This is a message for a Detective Howard? ...I'm, I'm, I'm returning your call concerning Emmett Boudin. Uh...I haven't seen Emmett in about a year. He left me his dog and that was the last time I saw him. But he always disappears for awhile, and then just shows up again... No one's ever reported him missing before. Uh...have you talked to his girlfriend?

Scene 6

(WESLEY crosses with a pair of walkie-talkies.)

WESLEY: We used to talk on these for hours...get lost in the woods...then look for each other..."What's your 10/20, Emmett?"...

(LIZA carries a piece of a door frame with pencil marks.)

LIZA: Emmett at two years old...Emmett at five...then six—

WESLEY: "Come on back."

LIZA: Seven…Emmett at twelve…

WESLEY: "Copy that."

LIZA: Emmett at fifteen…big jump there.

WESLEY: "Don't go too far."

LIZA: Emmett at eighteen…six feet tall.

WESLEY: "Roger, dodger."

LIZA: I'm not sure if he's grown since then…

WESLEY: "Over and out, good buddy. Over and out. Emmett?"

Scene 7

(SALLY *sits smoking.* HOWARD *sits across from her, the boots between them.*)

(*She has a shoe box on her lap.*)

HOWARD: Emmett Boudin lived with you, correct?

SALLY: Yes.

HOWARD: For how long?

SALLY: A year. On and off.

HOWARD: More on, or more off?

SALLY: On. I guess.

HOWARD: Were you lovers?
(*He waits.*)

(SALLY *smiles.*)

SALLY: What do you think?

HOWARD: I don't like to assume anything.
(*He nods, keeps looking at her.*)

SALLY: You want details?

HOWARD: No, no, that's quite alright.

SALLY: Then why are you staring at me?

HOWARD: Am I?

SALLY: Uh huh.

HOWARD: Sorry…I do that when I'm thinking…

SALLY: Were you thinking about Emmett and me in bed—

HOWARD: It's nothing personal. Just business…trying to connect the dots.

SALLY: Uh huh.

HOWARD: When was the last time you heard from him?

SALLY: You're still staring—

HOWARD: No, I'm done thinking about that. Now I'm just looking at you. When was the last time you heard from—

(SALLY *pulls her sweater tighter around her chest to cover herself.*)

SALLY: I don't know… Maybe eight months ago. Nine—

HOWARD: He call?

SALLY: Yes.

HOWARD: Where'd he call from?

SALLY: A pay phone.

HOWARD: He doesn't own a cell phone?

SALLY: No.

HOWARD: (Of course not.) Where was the pay phone?

SALLY: Nevada.

HOWARD: Where in Nevada?

SALLY: He didn't say.

HOWARD: Why not?

SALLY: I didn't ask.

HOWARD: Weren't you curious?

SALLY: Not really.

HOWARD: Why not?

SALLY: It's none of my business.

HOWARD: If there's a woman involved?

SALLY: *(Smiling)* Maybe.

HOWARD: What'd you talk about?

SALLY: The weather.

HOWARD: Look, I'm not the police.

SALLY: And I'm not his keeper.

(Silence)

HOWARD: What was he doing there?

SALLY: Where?

HOWARD: Nevada.

SALLY: He said he was making some money.

HOWARD: Doing what?

SALLY: Construction.

HOWARD: Is that how he usually makes his money?

SALLY: When he *makes* money…yes.

HOWARD: I see. Did he borrow from you?

SALLY: No.

HOWARD: Why not?

SALLY: I don't know. He just didn't.

HOWARD: Who's he get his money from?

SALLY: His grandmother mostly. Friends. Strangers. Women.

HOWARD: Women find that attractive?

SALLY: Have you seen a picture of Emmett?

HOWARD: Of course.

SALLY: People throw things at him.

HOWARD: Did you throw yourself at him?

SALLY: No.

HOWARD: Why not?

SALLY: I didn't have to.

(Silence)

HOWARD: Did he say where he was going next?

SALLY: No.

HOWARD: Did he consider coming back?

SALLY: Here?

HOWARD: Yes.

SALLY: No.

HOWARD: Why not?

SALLY: You ask too many questions.

HOWARD: Comes with the job. Did you end it?

SALLY: No.

HOWARD: What happened?

SALLY: None of your business.
(She puts out her cigarette.)

HOWARD: Are these his shoes?

(SALLY motions towards the box in her hands.)

SALLY: Here are some things you asked for. Things he gave me. Photos he took. Some notes he left. I don't know if they'll help.

HOWARD: You can take out the things you don't—

SALLY: I'm not sentimental.

(She's about to hand the box to HOWARD, *but stops—)*
His parents hired you, huh?

HOWARD: Yes.

SALLY: How'd they find you?

HOWARD: Internet.

SALLY: They think he's dead?

HOWARD: No. Missing.

SALLY: Missing from?

HOWARD: His family. They're worried he's—

SALLY: They've never been worried before. He disappears a lot. It's nothing unusual, you know.

HOWARD: Are these his shoes?

SALLY: He's never even had his own address.

HOWARD: That's what I hear.

SALLY: What makes them worry now?

HOWARD: No one knows where he is.

SALLY: That's the way he likes it.

HOWARD: Well. This isn't about what he likes now.

SALLY: He says his parents are assholes.

HOWARD: Maybe they did the best they could.

SALLY: Uh huh.

HOWARD: I hear he's pretty willful.

SALLY: What's wrong with that?

HOWARD: Nothing if it doesn't hurt anyone. But seems like he's bent on getting his way, doing whatever he wants, hurting people if he has to.

SALLY: That's bullshit.

HOWARD: Then why'd you hurt him?

(SALLY *quickly hands the box to* HOWARD.)

SALLY: Sorry I haven't been more help. I think you're wasting your time.

HOWARD: Are these his shoes?

SALLY: Yes.

(*Slides: random shots of abandoned houses, churches…*)

Scene 8

(LIZA *and* WESLEY *sit on a couch side-by-side, each holding an old photo of Emmett. Together, she is demure and polite; he, commander in chief of his household.*)

WESLEY: What the boy never really understood was discipline.

LIZA: That's not true.

WESLEY: He never buckled down.

LIZA: He was a state champion, got a scholarship.

WESLEY: That all went to hell, didn't it?

LIZA: Well. He--people change—

WESLEY: I'll say. The kid fell apart.

LIZA: Wesley—

WESLEY: It's true.

LIZA: You're too hard on him.

WESLEY: I should have been harder. Maybe show him some real strength. Some guts.

LIZA: He has courage. Look how he—

WESLEY: Wandering around like a vagrant. That's courage?

(*Silence*)

LIZA: He's not a vagrant.

WESLEY: What do you call it?

LIZA: I don't call it anything.

WESLEY: You babied him. That kid didn't know how to wipe his own ass.

LIZA: Wesley. Please.

WESLEY: You made him weak.

LIZA: I did no such thing.

WESLEY: *(To audience)* She really wanted a girl.

LIZA: Wesley, please don't make a scene—

WESLEY: You prayed for a girl. Every night. I heard you—

LIZA: It didn't matter—

WESLEY: "Please God...give me a little girl to love...a sweet little pink girl that I can dress up in fancy clothes to show off to my friends and who will do everything I say and look just pink and perfect all the time, Lord."

LIZA: I did no such thing—

WESLEY: He figured it out. The girl thing. And he hated you for it.

LIZA: He loves me.

WESLEY: He doesn't love anyone but himself.

LIZA: That's not true. He told me he loved me.

WESLEY: He's got a fine way of showing it.

LIZA: *(Whispers)* It's you he hates.
(Silence)
He was—is a kind boy. Talented. Everyone said so—

WESLEY: He was a great kid. I won't argue there—

LIZA: Thank you—

WESLEY: Then one day—bam—a pain in the ass. Hard-headed and unappreciative. A complete failure in everything.

LIZA: That's not true.

WESLEY: Sent him to college, and those liberal assholes stole his soul, littered his mind, stuffed him full of grandiose bull-shit ideas, and the so-called good times with my son, were over. Who did he decide he wanted to be when he grew up? A doctor? A lawyer? A fireman, maybe? No. No. Not him. I paid thirty thousand dollars year so he could graduate and become a fucking drifter.

LIZA: Wesley—

WESLEY: Why? Because once things got just a little bit hard, once he got just a taste of some real responsibility, just a taste of what it means to be a man, a real man in this world, he was done. Retired. Out of the loop. He didn't even *try to be more.* Why should he? You'd taught him it was better to be baby. It was easier to be a baby than a man. A pink baby doll—

LIZA: Shut up.
(She stands, she's had enough.)
(She glances apologetically at the audience before she exits.)

WESLEY: Walk out! Go ahead! Walk away from me!
(Silence)
See. There you have it. Witness for yourself. This family is officially full of crap. All of them.
(Shouts off stage)
Full of crap!
(He listens for a response.)
I break my back for these people, sell my soul to give them all the comforts in the world, and all of them turn on me. Show no respect. Mouth off. Don't call for four years. My mother dies. No letters… No remorse. Lies…

Blame… Like living with a bunch of pit bulls. Oh, they look like poodles, soft and pretty…but they're pit bulls. Don't be fooled. Their jaws will lock on your fucking heart at any minute. Takes a stick to beat them off.
(Silence)
I'm sick of it.
(He sits alone on the sofa. Unsure what to do next. He picks up the newspaper beside him.)

Scene 9

(JOHN sits on a back pack. He pulls a journal from the top. [He wears a pair of expensive sunglasses.])

JOHN: "The individual has always had to struggle to keep from being overwhelmed by the tribe."
(He keeps reading.)
"Must eat more leafy greens."
(Unimpressed, he keeps reading.)
"The greatest revolution of our generation is the discovery that human beings, by changing the inner attitudes of their minds, can change the outer aspects of their lives."
(He shakes his head.)
Right.
(He sighs and turns the page. He continues reading through the journal, looking for something interesting.)
"Arkansas. Tuesday the 4th. Today I saw a long stretch of highway and nothing but a shadow, (mine, I think), my feet walking, and an abandoned doll. She was face up to the sky. I picked her up and carried her with me. She had long blond hair, (tangled), blue eyes that didn't close, and a frozen smile. She was naked. I put an old T-shirt on her and left her in the ladies room of the first gas station I came to. Seemed the proper thing

to do. Although now, as I'm sitting here in the dark, I miss her. Her smile was resigned, but comforting."
(He turns another page. A pressed flower falls out. He smells it.)

Scene 10

(MIRANDA enters, holding a set of keys.)

MIRANDA: I was looking for someone at the time. I was bordering on desperate, but I was trying very hard to hide it. I would sit on my hands some nights, just to keep them still. Keep them from grabbing someone... Dragging him home with me... Panic was setting in. I'd just had my forty-third birthday and I could feel my body saying good-bye to my last eggs. I could literally feel my body giving up. Throwing in the towel. Settling. For a future of quiet. Emptiness. Old age and loneliness. All the things I never wanted, but suddenly found myself.... Living with... And I was scared to death that This was it. My life... Signed and sealed, with no one else it in...I didn't know what happened. I swear, one day I went to bed twenty-four, and the next morning I woke up forty-three. And I really can't tell you where all the years went, but I think I enjoyed them. I think I did. I mean, I made a career for myself. I bought a house. I traveled some. I ate good food. Drank good, expensive wine. Indulged... And there was love in there, and sex, and some promises made involving forever, and some plans made, but nothing that really stuck. Nothing that really Had to be. So they weren't, and they didn't, and we didn't, and I never got around to saying Stay. So they didn't...I was alone. It was getting late...Emmett was sitting next to me at the bar and he needed a place to stay for the night, so I said please. Sure. Please. Gosh. Of course. Come on over. Please. Stay as long as you want.

Scene 11

(JOHN continues with the journal.)

JOHN: "We must travel in the direction of our fear"
(He turns a few pages.)
"I now hate the word "Freedom". It's covered in blood.
And oil. (Turns out, they mix.)"
*(He turns another page. He stops and looks closer at the
bottom of the page.)*
"Las Vegas"
*(He pulls a pair of long fake eyelashes from the page, and
carefully puts them on each eye.)*

*(LIZA and WESLEY struggle to carry a twin bed across stage
as JOHN reads from the journal.* Star Wars *sheets drag off
the bed as they carry it off.)*

JOHN: "I turned thirty last week and sometimes all
I want is for someone else to tie my shoes. Kiss my
forehead. Tuck me into bed someplace safe."
(He turns the page.)
"Some words to use more often:
sincerely
valiant
trespass
perhaps
radiant
splendid
super-duper
love
ghastly
woebegone
Indeed!"
(He turns the page again. An old bar napkin falls out.)
"Silence is argument carried out by other means."

Scene 12

(HOWARD *has the box of* SALLY's *things, the boots on a table. He studies a map of the United States. He's adding colored pins to various locations.*)

HOWARD: Okay, folks. This is what we've got. One box of Hallmark cards and snapshots, two boots...
(He takes a good long look at the map.)
And a whole lot of women.
(He takes out his pointer, to point out various parts of the U S.)
I have learned that Mr Emmett Boudin had a lady-friend here...and here...and here...and here...and here... Obviously, Mr Boudin can get by on his good looks. His so called, "charm". (The kid has the eyes of a fawn, the soul of a jackrabbit.)
(He clears his throat. Takes a swig of coffee)
His grandmother Ruth, paternal grandmother, died in October. Now I wonder if that had some kind of impact on the kid. Because from what I can gather, he quickly went from here
(Points to Michigan)
To here.
(Points to South Dakota)
To here
(Points to Texas)
Her other grand kids say Ruth favored Emmett. Say Emmett was closer to her than his parents. Some of them were a little jealous. Say that he drained her bank account more than she would let on... From the Western Union receipts, he did get quite a bit of aid. Two nundred dollars here...fifty bucks there...it added up.
(He studies the map. Scratches his head)

What I can't figure out, is how Mr Emmett Boudin
learned of his grandmother's death. No one in the
family claims they've heard from him in over four
years, and thus, no one sent word of her passing. How
did he get this information? One of her friends? The
internet? ...Perhaps... Why did he come to California?
The boots were here in Los Angeles. Why? I don't
think he stuck around here. The kid hated cities.
(He takes another sip of coffee.)
Did he go South? Mexico? South America? North to
Alaska? Head back East where he had friends? Did he
go to his grandmother's grave? (Possibly. I'll look into
that.)
(He jots a quick note on a pad of paper from his pocket.)
Did he go overseas? His cousin said he was always
afraid of airplanes as a kid... And it doesn't seem his
style... Too expensive...
*(He gets lost in his own thoughts. Checks the notes in his
pad.)*
From what I've learned about him he's always broke...
but proud... He's a self-proclaimed woodsman...
Quiet. Funny. Lean. Left-handed. Allergic to cats.
He's got a scar over his right eye from a skateboard
accident in fifth grade. He smokes. He's athletic. Great
with babies. Better with dogs. Bad with authority.
Spiritually inclined. Idealistic. Moody. Unpredictable.
Goofy. Serene. Unremarkable. Unreliable. "Scar is
over his *left* eye." Scared of babies. Pot head. Clean-
cut. Deranged. Devoted. Lovely. Sad. Fantastic. Free-
spirited. Lost. Bold. Confused. Always Absolutely One
Hundred Percent Certain.

Scene 13

(LIZA *walks across the stage with a handful of stuffed animals.*)

(WESLEY *walks across with a B B gun, as if he's hunting* LIZA *and the animals.*)

Scene 14

(MIRANDA *stands with a baby sleeping in sling across her chest.*)

(HOWARD *sits with a pad of paper on his lap.*)

MIRANDA: Can I get you anything, Mr Howard? Cup of coffee. Tea?

HOWARD: No thank you. I'm fine. Nice house.

MIRANDA: Thank you. Are you sure? It wouldn't take but a minute. I made some cookies last night—

HOWARD: I'm trying to watch my weight.

MIRANDA: Oh. Well, you look fine to me.

HOWARD: Tell that to my wife.
(*Gesturing toward the baby*)
What's his/her name?

MIRANDA: His. Joe.

HOWARD: Nice. Solid name.

MIRANDA: Are you sure you don't want something? A glass of water? I really seems rude to just let you sit there empty-handed—

HOWARD: I'm fine. When was the last time you talked to Emmett?

MIRANDA: Well, let me see…five months ago.

HOWARD: Did he call?

MIRANDA: No, he came home.

HOWARD: He did?

MIRANDA: We had a baby.

HOWARD: This is his son?

MIRANDA: You looked surprised.

HOWARD: His parents didn't mention a grandchild.

MIRANDA: They didn't?

HOWARD: No. No, they did not.
(He takes a note.)

MIRANDA: Emmett told me he sent them a picture.

HOWARD: No.
(Silence)
Do you know where Emmett is now?

MIRANDA: Oh. No. No. I'm sorry, I don't.

HOWARD: Are you worried?

MIRANDA: Should I be?

HOWARD: That's what I'm trying to find out.

MIRANDA: He really isn't one to call. Or check in. Not with me anyway.

HOWARD: Does that bother you?

MIRANDA: Uh. Well, yes. Sometimes. But you know, it doesn't help to worry.

HOWARD: Why do you think he doesn't call, check in?

MIRANDA: We're not married.

HOWARD: What, you have to be married to be considerate?

MIRANDA: No, but—

HOWARD: Would you like to be married?

MIRANDA: The baby has my last name.

HOWARD: So you've discussed it?
(*He takes a note.*)

MIRANDA: Are you sure I can't at least take your coat—

HOWARD: I'm fine.

MIRANDA: A private investigator. Sounds like interesting work.

HOWARD: Sometimes.

MIRANDA: Exciting?

HOWARD: Tedious is more like it. Was the baby planned?

MIRANDA: Yes.
(*Silence*)
So people hire you to find other people. Anywhere in the United States.

HOWARD: Yes.

MIRANDA: How?

HOWARD: Any way I can.

MIRANDA: And you've been hired to find Emmett?
(*She smiles.*)
Oh boy.

HOWARD: Why is that everyone, except his parents, seems to show absolutely no concern that he's missing?

MIRANDA: Missing?

HOWARD: Yes.

MIRANDA: If you know Emmett well enough, you would never think he's missing. Never. He's just… away.

HOWARD: What's the difference?

MIRANDA: He's coming back. He always comes back. At some point. It's just physically and emotionally impossible for him to commit to one place.

HOWARD: Or person?

(*Silence*)

There's a Prince Charming.

MIRANDA: He wants to experience as many things as possible.

HOWARD: Uh huh—

MIRANDA: He has ideals. Ideals he wants to understand and explore. I admire him—

HOWARD: What kind of ideals?

MIRANDA: Adventure. America. The ride into the sunset.

HOWARD: (Goddamn Jack Kerouac.)

MIRANDA: I would have done it at his age, if I had the courage.

HOWARD: He's thirty years old.

MIRANDA: Twenty-five.

HOWARD: Thirty. He's the father of your child but he took off. Left you alone with a new baby. No help. No sense of responsibility—

MIRANDA: I never asked Emmett to be responsible. I asked him to be here when the baby was born. That's it. I didn't ask him for anything else. I'm a capable person—

HOWARD: I see.

MIRANDA: I'm not trying to put a leash on anyone.

HOWARD: My apologies.

MIRANDA: That was never my intention.

HOWARD: But surely, you were hoping…maybe hoping just a little, that once he saw that baby, once he saw his son, he'd—

MIRANDA: No.

HOWARD: I suppose I just assume a few things—I assume most men feel a responsibility to their children. And the women who—

MIRANDA: Not everyone's looking for the picket fence.

HOWARD: Or they've lost faith in it.
(Silence)
My wife and I did alright. With most of it. Some of it.

MIRANDA: Well, I don't need the fence. I'm happy to just get the truth from someone, and maybe a bundle of flowers every now and then.

HOWARD: That's it?

MIRANDA: I got a son.

HOWARD: No strings attached?

MIRANDA: No.

HOWARD: Not one?

MIRANDA: No.

HOWARD: You're sure? Not even one string? A thread maybe? One thread?

(MIRANDA smiles, changing the subject.)

MIRANDA: Do you need anything else, Mr Howard?

HOWARD: Any idea why Emmett would be in L A?

MIRANDA: No.

HOWARD: Do you mind if I look through Emmett's personal belongings?

MIRANDA: I'm not sure if he'd appreciate that—

HOWARD: Look, his parents are worried about their son. You understand that.

MIRANDA: It's not much. Just a bag in the back bedroom.

HOWARD: I'm going to need to take it with me.

MIRANDA: He is coming back for it.

HOWARD: He can contact me.

MIRANDA: He won't be happy about it. He's a pretty private person, Mr Howard. He doesn't like his things—

HOWARD: I'd be thrilled to hear from him.

MIRANDA: I'm getting the impression you don't really like Emmett very much, Mr Howard.

HOWARD: Really?

MIRANDA: Yes.

HOWARD: Huh.

MIRANDA: That doesn't seem very helpful to your… case.

HOWARD: Let's just say, I know these type of young men. I've dealt with them before.

MIRANDA: Personally?

HOWARD: Yes.

MIRANDA: Then you know there's really nothing to worry about.
(Silence)
Right?

HOWARD: If you'll excuse me, I've got work to do. Time is not my friend in this business.
(He exits.)

(MIRANDA *sits down. The baby begins to cry.)*

(Music)

(Slides: truck stops. Etc)

Scene 15

(LIZA *steals a moment. She has a drawing of Emmett's beside her. It's stick figures of two large parents and one very little boy.*)

LIZA: Here's the thing…. And please…please, I would really like to apologize for my husband's behavior earlier. Please excuse us.

(She straightens her perfectly straight skirt.)

It's not at all polite to be forced to sit there and watch us squabble…I'm sorry. Not at all polite. I don't like that kind of behavior one bit, not one bit, but…but, my husband and I often disagree on what is proper, what is polite… He was raised by Carnies, you see…well, not necessarily carnies, but close— "Bohemians" … and he never did learn to consider the feelings of those around him…anything for a laugh or argument with that group…all emotion, no tact…no restraint… My father was a minister, and manners were very, very important in our household, very important, expected, and well, *(Sighs)* I don't know why Wesley caught my eye but he did. I was young and foolish and he came to my high school and he was, he seemed so handsome and exotic and "interesting"…

(She shakes her head at her own stupidity…)

Well.

(She checks to see if anyone's coming.)

As you might imagine, this has all been very difficult, very painful for us…to be abandoned by our own son. To be shut out for all these years, and for the life of me, I can't figure out what we've done to deserve this… Not once did I ever hit Emmett…I never spanked him and I would not let Wesley lay a hand on him either… not in my house…there was yelling, (with a man like Wesley, you can imagine) but never violence. Never.

(Silence)

I don't know what happened to us...to my family...I
really don't...I don't know what to make of the man
that my son has became, this stranger, and why he
disappeared and if he has any idea how hurtful it's
been to be forgotten, to be shut out...I just had—have
one...one child...that's all I could have...one...twenty-
four hours of labor for seven pounds eight ounces of
one son...and now I have nothing but four years of
silence and an angry husband and a very big hole in
my life. I'm afraid it's going to swallow us both—

WESLEY: (O S) Liza? What are you jabbering on about
out there?

(LIZA *gathers herself. Pushes a smile*)

LIZA: Well.

(LIZA *and* MIRANDA *exit at the same time.*)

Scene 16

ROOSTER: He hit me in the back of the head with his
pencil. Then he hit me in the back of the head with
his eraser. Then his lunch box. Then his shoe. Then
his other shoe. Then his notebook. Math book. Big
thick science book. Some girl's retainer. Another kid's
headgear. A banana. An apple. A box of crayons.
Anything anyone would give him. A Luke Skywalker
action figure. Princess Lea. Lip gloss. A rabbit's foot.
Raisins... Boogers... Names... Giggles... Farts...
Feathers...I swear, I felt it all...When he ran out of
things from others to throw, he had to resort back to
his own stuff, his Miami Dolphins jacket. His favorite
socks. His Miami Dolphins T-shirt...And he was
furious at this point... Livid... Seething... Because I
wouldn't turn around...I absolutely refused to turn
around.... He was so worked up, so pissed off that I
was ignoring him, ignoring the most popular kid in

seventh grade, ignoring everything he hit me with,
even his favorite T-shirt, that he finally had to just
get up and drag me out of my desk to punch me in
the fucking nose. He'd had enough. He was going
to smack me in the nose, he was going to get it over
with... Show me, really show me, when to turn
around for Emmett Boudin. When to let him get my
attention.... But... Then he saw my face. He saw that
I was crying. That my whole face was covered in tears
and snot. My lips were quivering....I was a fucking
mess. And so his ready-to-punch me-in-the-nose-arm,
his right hook, hung there, in mid-air. Just hung there
as he realized he'd made me cry. Cry like a little baby.
Everyone was laughing, but him... Everyone was
pointing and egging him on, but he wasn't listening...
We sat there on the classroom floor staring at each
other, me in tears, and him ashamed, beginning to cry
himself. We sat there establishing a pact. The secret
pact of cry babies. He grabbed my hand, helped me
up, and together we walked out to recess, never saying
another word about it. From that point on, we were
inseparable.

Scene 17

(WESLEY *carries a hand-made sign across the stage that
reads: "For the Love of God, Keep out of my room, Mom and
Dad!"*)

(HOWARD *carries a duffel bag in the opposite direction.*)

Scene 18

(Music: a song like Keep on the Sunny Side of Life *plays.)*

(JOHN surrounds himself with his new treasures: Emmett's things. He wears Emmett's walkman, grooving to the music, trying on the hats, clothes, etc, as he unpacks them from the pack:)

(A Nikon camera)

(A video camera)

(Worn paperback books)

(Letters)

(Two stocking hats)

(3 flannel shirts)

(2 pair khaki pants)

(Underwear)

(2 pair of socks)

(A baby photo)

(A pack of cigarettes, half-smoked)

(A yellow pancho)

(A Swiss Army knife)

(Shaving cream)

(Toothbrush. Toothpaste)

(A mirror)

(Old Spice deodorant)

(A camping stove)

(A deck of worn Tarot cards)

(A down vest)

(A bag of pot. [He gives that a welcome smell])

(A stack of yellow legal pads)

(2 pens)

(A baby's sock)

(A box of crayons)

(A roll of toilet paper)

(A gun)

Scene 19

(ROOSTER *enters with the dog on a leash and a camping chair.* HOWARD *meets him in the middle of the stage.)*

HOWARD: Rooster. Detective Howard. Nice to meet you.

ROOSTER: I thought you were a Private Investigator?

HOWARD: Same thing.

(HOWARD *and* ROOSTER *shake hands.)*

HOWARD: Nice dog.
(He pats the dog's head.)
Does he do any tricks?

ROOSTER: He licks himself.

(ROOSTER *offers* HOWARD *the seat.)*

ROOSTER: Please.

HOWARD: Thank you for taking the time to meet with me.

ROOSTER: Sure. Yeah. Anything. Yeah. Of course.

HOWARD: *(Taking in the chair)* Wow. Isn't this comfortable.
(He enjoys his seat.)
You know, camping is much more luxurious than it used to be. I mean, look at this, for Christ's sake. Cup holders. In the chair. Everything's got cup holders

now. When I was a kid, we had to sit on the dirt and hold our own drinks.

ROOSTER: I guess things change—

HOWARD: Bug spray on everyone. Air-mattresses. Satellite television. D V D players. You name it. You can live like a king outside now, huh?

ROOSTER: If you want.

HOWARD: You got a nice set up?

ROOSTER: What do you mean?

HOWARD: You have M T V and E S P N and all that?

ROOSTER: I've got a cabin—

HOWARD: Heat?

ROOSTER: Yeah.

HOWARD: Jesus.

ROOSTER: Well, I have a girlfriend. She likes that. It's a wood stove. So...yeah. It's a nice—

HOWARD: I met Emmett's girlfriend.

ROOSTER: Which one?

HOWARD: Well, a few of them. Thanks for the names.

ROOSTER: Sure, sure.

HOWARD: Met that Sally. She's a looker, huh?

ROOSTER: Sure.

HOWARD: And he's got a kid with Miranda.

ROOSTER: Really?

HOWARD: He didn't tell you?

ROOSTER: No.

HOWARD: Yeah. Five months. Boy. Named him Joe.

ROOSTER: Wow.

HOWARD: Does that surprise you?

ROOSTER: Uh. Yes. No. No. I guess not.

HOWARD: So it's no big deal he's left a son?

ROOSTER: How do you know he's left him?

HOWARD: You think he's alive and well?

ROOSTER: Why wouldn't I?

HOWARD: Then where is he?

ROOSTER: I don't know. You're, you're the detective, sir.

(Silence)

HOWARD: I saw your letters.

(ROOSTER pets the dog.)

HOWARD: Miranda gave me his things. He left a stack of letters. To friends. His grandmother. From you. And other people. Doesn't sound like he answered them.

ROOSTER: He wasn't very good about correspondence.

HOWARD: But you kept writing? There were more letters from you than anyone else.

ROOSTER: He's my best friend.

HOWARD: His grandmother died. Did you know that?

(Silence)

ROOSTER: No.

HOWARD: He didn't talk to you about it?

ROOSTER: No.

HOWARD: You think it might have something to do with his disappearance?

ROOSTER: I don't think he's disappeared. Sir. Not for good—

HOWARD: Why not?

ROOSTER: Why would I want to think that?

HOWARD: Does that thought scare you?

ROOSTER: Of course.

HOWARD: Rooster—what kind of name is that anyway?

ROOSTER: I used to have red hair as a kid. It stuck up.

HOWARD: My son had a friend with red hair. Pale skin. Freckles. He was afraid of the sun.

ROOSTER: I'm not afraid of the sun—

HOWARD: Why are you trying to protect Emmett? Is he in trouble?

ROOSTER: I'm not—I, I don't know. I really have no idea—

HOWARD: Sounds like he called you a few times.

ROOSTER: He did.

HOWARD: Where was he?

ROOSTER: He wouldn't tell me.

HOWARD: Why not?

ROOSTER: He thinks it's cute.

HOWARD: Thinks what's cute?

ROOSTER: To be mysterious.

HOWARD: What do you think?

ROOSTER: About what?

HOWARD: Emmett's lifestyle.

ROOSTER: I think he should be able to live the way that he wants. It's his life.

HOWARD: True. True enough.

ROOSTER: Leave him to it.

(HOWARD *gets out of the chair.*)

HOWARD: Your letters are a little more explicit.

ROOSTER: Are they?

HOWARD: You told him you hated him.

ROOSTER: *(Laughs)* I don't remember that.

HOWARD: You did.

ROOSTER: I was probably kidding.

HOWARD: You told him that he used people wherever he went.

ROOSTER: He does.

HOWARD: You told him it was time to grow up.

ROOSTER: *(Shrugs)* He's lazy.

HOWARD: You told him to stop calling you.

ROOSTER: Did I?

HOWARD: Yes.

ROOSTER: Why would I do that?

HOWARD: I don't know.

ROOSTER: He's my best friend.

HOWARD: Maybe you're jealous?

ROOSTER: Of what?

HOWARD: He doesn't need a cabin. Fancy chairs with cup holders. A warm girl.

ROOSTER: So?

HOWARD: Maybe you wish you were him.

ROOSTER: Why would I wish that?

HOWARD: What about Sally?

ROOSTER: What about her?

HOWARD: Emmett has everything he needs on his back.

ROOSTER: I have thousands of acres here—

HOWARD: He has the world at his feet—

ROOSTER: So do I—

HOWARD: He doesn't care about anyone but himself—

ROOSTER: So—

HOWARD: And look at all the things he's seen. The adventures. The freedom. What a life.

ROOSTER: I think mine's pretty good.

HOWARD: Really?

ROOSTER: What do you want?

HOWARD: Obviously, Rooster, I want to know where he is.

ROOSTER: I don't know where he is. I'm sorry.

HOWARD: But I think you might have an idea.

ROOSTER: And I'd be keeping that information from you because...?

HOWARD: Does Emmett have a girlfriend in L A?

ROOSTER: I don't know—

HOWARD: You think Emmett would take his own life?

ROOSTER: No.

HOWARD: Why not?

ROOSTER: He's not a depressive personality. Believe me.

HOWARD: No?

ROOSTER: No.

HOWARD: People change.

ROOSTER: Everybody loves him. And he knows it.

HOWARD: Why? Why does everybody love him?

ROOSTER: He's just...just one of those people. I can't explain it. He becomes the center of everything.

HOWARD: *(Confidentially)* Personally, I think he sounds like a jerk.

ROOSTER: You wouldn't think that if you met him.

HOWARD: How do you know?

ROOSTER: He'd have you buying him a drink in two minutes.

HOWARD: I'm cheap.

ROOSTER: But he'd make you feel like you were the most interesting person that he'd ever talked to. He could make you feel…brilliant. Then he'd make you laugh. And he'd make you feel like everything was just so possible in the world, that it was time for a drink to celebrate this new friendship. Four drinks later, the whole bar has gathered around and he's the party and everyone high because they too can conquer world hunger or climb Mt. Everest, and they want to shake his hand and hug him and help Emmett anyway they can.

HOWARD: What if I don't drink?

ROOSTER: You'd start.
(He pets the dog.)
And the next thing you know, he's "gotta go, man", and you're offering to keep his dog.

HOWARD: He could have got in trouble.

(Silence)

ROOSTER: Maybe.

HOWARD: He could have crossed the wrong person. Someone who didn't want to share the party.

ROOSTER: Look. I care about him—

HOWARD: This is a dangerous country. Weird shit happens every minute of the day.

ROOSTER: Yeah—

HOWARD: People get tangled in tragic situations—

ROOSTER: Emmett is better at avoiding difficult situations than getting tangled up in them, believe me—

HOWARD: Things happen fast.

ROOSTER: Please--will you please stop--I feel like you're treating me like I'm guilty of something.

HOWARD: Am I?

ROOSTER: I'm his friend. I love him.

HOWARD: Okay.

ROOSTER: And as his friend, I know if you wait a few months, he'll turn up. He always does. He's probably just out on some silent retreat or herding cattle or something stupid like that. And honestly, if Emmett's parents hired you, and are suddenly so anxious to find Emmett, they must want something. They're the ones you should be questioning.

HOWARD: Why?

ROOSTER: There's a reason they want their son home.

HOWARD: Other than the normal reasons most parents would want their only son home after years of—

ROOSTER: Those two always have an agenda.

HOWARD: Most people have an agenda.

ROOSTER: Some people. Maybe—

HOWARD: It's either work. Sex. Happiness. Revenge. Money. Jealousy—

ROOSTER: But some don't, Mr Howard—

HOWARD: Power. Bravery. Fame. Fortune. Adventure. Jealousy. Love. Even Love is an agenda.

ROOSTER: Maybe.

HOWARD: It is. Think what people will do for it.

(ROOSTER *begins to fold the chair.*)

ROOSTER: I've got to get back to work—

(HOWARD *grabs* ROOSTER's *arm.*)

HOWARD: What happened to your best friend?

ROOSTER: Take your hands off me.

(ROOSTER *waits for* HOWARD *to take remove his hands.*)

ROOSTER: You're asking the wrong person. Sir.

(ROOSTER *whistles, and the dog follows him off stage.*)

Scene 20

(WESLEY *has a large box, begins to keep walking, but stops.*)

WESLEY: This bears mentioning.

(*He sets down the box and opens a year book.*)

This is what the kid *was*. Okay. Class president.

(*He turns a few pages.*)

Captain of the track team.

(*He turns more pages.*)

"Most likely to succeed".

(*He puts the yearbook aside.*)

That was just his senior year.

(*He pulls a trophy from the box.*)

Junior year. State Champion. Cross country.

(*He studies the trophy.*)

First place.

(*He touches the name on the brass plate.*)

My son. My boy.

(*Catches himself, edging toward sentiment… He quickly places the trophy back in the box.*)

He could do anything.

(*He finds an old baseball glove.*)

I mean.

(*He finds a small baseball hat.*)

Anything.

(WESLEY *puts the glove back and picks up the box and continues across the stage, bumping into* LIZA, *as she carries an arm-load of books across the stage, books of every size, shape, subject.*)

LIZA: These are what really did him in: Emerson. Nietzche. Buddha. Marx—

(HOWARD *interrupts them, setting down the boots, and pulling out his note pad.*)

HOWARD: Anything else?

(LIZA *looks at* WESLEY.)

LIZA: No.

HOWARD: Nothing more I should know?

LIZA: Not that I can think of.

WESLEY: No.

(LIZA *and* WESLEY *continue off stage, leaving* HOWARD *alone.*)

HOWARD: Why Los Angeles?! ...I really need more, folks—
(*He puts away his note pad, frustrated, and looks at the boots on the floor.*)
(*He slips off his shoes, and puts on the boots. [They fit.]*)
(*He picks up his old shoes, and walks off stage.*)

(*Music*)

END OF ACT ONE

ACT TWO

Scene 1

(SALLY *enters in nothing but a towel.*)

SALLY: Every time he'd come back to me, he'd taste of
all the places he'd been. His lips, his hair, his skin, held
everything he'd done, seen, thought, ate, drank, loved.
He could hide nothing from me, and worse, I guess,
he never tried. There were things I was happy to taste.
Like pine needles and maple leaves, apple blossoms,
oranges, coffee, wood and tobacco smoke. Bourbon; my
favorite sweet, warm whiskey. I would hope I'd taste
those things. And there were things I never minded:
Tar, asphalt, rail road dirt, sweat, worry, gasoline,
snow, rain. Rain I liked, actually. A storm was exciting.
And the things I minded. The things I didn't like,
that I wanted to wash from him. Scrub him for days:
the perfume, the lipstick, silly laughs, strange sheets
on fancy beds, condoms, and other things you can
imagine. But. Well. I guess he could taste those things
on me too that he didn't want, that sank his heart and
sent a thousand pictures to his mind that he didn't ask
to see. A silence would suddenly descend upon us.
Because the deal we struck, the deal we thought was
fair to both of us, while we were apart, was actually
just a bad taste of the loneliness we were both trying
to fill. There was nothing to say about that. So I would
bring us both a glass of wine, we'd proceed to drink
two bottles, and then we'd take a shower together.

We'd stay in there until the water ran cold. Drunk and shivering we'd climb into bed. And somehow, that was enough to break the silence. And pull up our hearts a little. So we could begin again. For awhile.

Scene 2

(HOWARD *enters.* SALLY *remains in her towel.)*

SALLY: I wish you would have called.

HOWARD: I was in the neighborhood.

(SALLY *exits to put on a robe.)*

SALLY: *(O S)* You just crossed four States, Howard.

HOWARD: I see you and Rooster still talk.

(SALLY *enters.)*

SALLY: You get around.

HOWARD: So do you.

SALLY: You get lonely, driving around the country, looking for clues?

HOWARD: Is that a come on?

SALLY: I'm not into old guys.

HOWARD: Neither is my wife.

SALLY: Maybe she's tired of you chasing down women. Not coming home.

HOWARD: Maybe.

SALLY: You and Emmett have a lot in common.

HOWARD: Maybe. I never thought about it.

SALLY: Roaming men. Full of questions. With a horrible sense of fashion.

(HOWARD *inspects his rumpled clothes.)*

SALLY: Why are you wearing Emmett's shoes?

HOWARD: They fit. You didn't tell me about Rooster.

SALLY: I didn't think it mattered. That's weird.

HOWARD: They're comfortable. It mattered to Emmett.

SALLY: That was years ago.

HOWARD: It seems to have had an impact.

SALLY: Not really. We both moved on.

HOWARD: Of course. Everyone moves on.

SALLY: He has lots of girls. And now I hear he has a kid with someone. Believe me, I was just one among many.

HOWARD: You think so?

SALLY: Yeah—

(HOWARD *throws a ring box in* SALLY's *lap.*)

SALLY: How do you know it's for me?

HOWARD: It's engraved.

(SALLY *opens it.*)

HOWARD: "Marry me, Sally girl." ...It was in his stuff at Miranda's house.

SALLY: Who's Miranda?

HOWARD: The mother of his son.

SALLY: Oh.
(Silence)
I never knew her name.
(Silence)
Is she pretty?

HOWARD: Yes.

(Silence)

SALLY: Prettier than me?

HOWARD: I don't know.

SALLY: So she is.

HOWARD: No.

(SALLY *nods.*)

SALLY: What does she think?

HOWARD: About what?

SALLY: Him. You. This "hunt". What does she think?

HOWARD: You want to talk to her?

SALLY: Why'd you give me this?

HOWARD: I thought you might like to know—

SALLY: Why? What good does it do me?

HOWARD: I don't know…I thought it might help put a piece of the puzzle together—

SALLY: I'm not a fucking piece of a puzzle. I hate to break it to you, but I'm not that complicated. I'm just some girl he lived with.

(SALLY *hands* HOWARD *back the ring.*)

SALLY: This doesn't mean anything.

HOWARD: You believe that?

SALLY: He didn't give it to me.

HOWARD: Would you have taken it?

SALLY: What difference does it make? He didn't give it to me.

HOWARD: Would you have taken it?

SALLY: Ask him.

HOWARD: I'd like to. I'd like to. I'd like to ask him a lot of things. But…I need to find him to do that.

SALLY: He didn't—he didn't kill himself over of me, Mr Howard. If that's what you're here for. If that's what you think—

HOWARD: How do you know?

SALLY: He didn't love me that much. And he faints at the sight of blood.

HOWARD: He loved you enough to want to marry you.

SALLY: That's just a gesture.

HOWARD: Of?

SALLY: Someone he'd like to be.

HOWARD: Maybe you're wrong.

SALLY: You find an engagement ring and think you've found a romantic.

HOWARD: I did—

SALLY: Look deeper, and you might find someone else. Emmett would like to be a lot of things.

HOWARD: Like what?

SALLY: You name it—

HOWARD: I need specifics! Isn't there anything *specific* that he wants from his fucking life? Was there any kind of plan? Direction? Dreams?

SALLY: Yeah, well, he's not too good with specifics. He wants to do something great and important. He just can't seem to narrow down his...legacy.

(SALLY *watches as* HOWARD *looks at the ring. Puts it in his pocket*)

HOWARD: I'll be honest with you...I'm struggling here...I've got some stuff, some women, some names, but no real clues.... His parents are stuck in the past. Helpless. I've got no footprints. Nothing and no one with any concrete evidence of his whereabouts...these boots were just a fluke, a lucky tip... But nothing else. It doesn't make sense.
(*Silence*)
I don't know where to go next.

SALLY: Try his grandmother's. That's where he always went when he didn't know where to go next.

HOWARD: She's dead.

SALLY: Does Emmett know she's dead?

HOWARD: I think so.

(Silence)

Why was she so important?

SALLY: She loved him.

HOWARD: So do you.

SALLY: She loved him unconditionally.

HOWARD: And you don't?

SALLY: You think you're so sly.

(Silence)

HOWARD: Well. I've lost him.

(Silence)

SALLY: Did you try the morgues?

HOWARD: Hell.

SALLY: Did you?

HOWARD: How long do you think I've been doing this?

SALLY: I don't know—

HOWARD: Of course.

SALLY: That's good. That's good news, right? That's great news—

HOWARD: You know how many dead John Doe's are sitting rotting in morgues in this country?

SALLY: A lot?

(Silence)

HOWARD: This is a depressing job.

SALLY: Why do you do it?

HOWARD: I have my reasons.

SALLY: What are they?

(HOWARD *studies the ceiling, points.*)

HOWARD: You should get that leak fixed, you know. That'll rot the shit out of your house.

SALLY: Can I have my ring back?

(HOWARD *hands* SALLY *back the ring box.*)

(SALLY *takes out the ring, reads it again, and puts it on.*)

SALLY: One night I came home and Emmett was laying on the couch, staring at the ceiling. Just staring. He didn't turn to look at me when I came in, didn't say hello. He just kept staring. I tried to get his attention…I sat on him, I kissed him, I finally put my face between his and the ceiling, and asked him, "What the hell? Jesus." Finally, he said, "I think you have a leak in the roof. Right there."
(Silence)
It was lonely to be with Emmett. Wonderful then lonely. Rooster understood that side of him…so, when I didn't want to feel lonely anymore, and I knew Emmett was coming home early, well…I wanted to end that feeling.

HOWARD: My wife has mentioned that. Feeling.

SALLY: It's awful.

HOWARD: So I'm told.

SALLY: You know there's all this great stuff in there, and occasionally you'd get a peek at it—just big enough to keep you wanting more; a question no one else has asked you before, a sweet note, a look, a hug that lasts longer than you thought it would. But he won't let you have the rest, and you begin to hate him for hoarding the good stuff, and giving you the fucking leak in the roof.

(Silence)

*(*HOWARD *stands.)*

HOWARD: Well. I guess I've taken enough of your time. It's been nice talking to you.
(He offers his hand.)
Well, take care of yourself, kid.

SALLY: You don't think he's dead, do you?

HOWARD: I hope not.
(He begins to exit—)

SALLY: Wait. Uh. Just. Wait.
(She exits and returns with a video tape.)
Emmett sent this to me.

HOWARD: When?

SALLY: February.

HOWARD: It's March, Sally.

*(*SALLY *hands* HOWARD *the video.)*

HOWARD: Did you have this last time I saw you?

SALLY: I guess I hoard a few things too.

Scene 3

(Music)

(Video: montage of Santa Monica beach)

Scene 4

*(*HOWARD *has* JOHN *by the T-shirt, dragging him on stage with one hand, Emmett's pack with the other. He rips the sunglasses from* JOHN'S *face.)*

HOWARD: Got yourself a whole new get up, huh.

JOHN: Nothing new…no.

HOWARD: The glasses?

JOHN: Found 'em.

HOWARD: The video camera?

JOHN: Found.

HOWARD: The pack, books, sleeping bag, letters, clothes—

JOHN: Found found found found found found.

HOWARD: You're quite the pirate.

JOHN: Ay.

HOWARD: Don't be smart.

JOHN: I can't help it.

(HOWARD *picks up one of Emmett's shirts from the pack. Looks at it closely. Smells it. Then holds up a pair of his old khaki pants. [Creates an odd portrait with the empty set of clothes. Lays them on the stage, and that creates another odd portrait of an empty man on the ground.]*)

JOHN: What's your deal?

(HOWARD *just stares at the clothes.*)

JOHN: Hey, man—hey, why do you get to wear the boots?

HOWARD: Did you see Mr Boudin alive?

JOHN: That's not fair, man—

HOWARD: *(Louder)* Did you see him alive?

(JOHN *shrugs.*)

HOWARD: Is that a yes?

(JOHN *shrugs again.*)

JOHN: Affirmative.

HOWARD: When?

(JOHN *shrugs again.*)

HOWARD: When?

JOHN: I don't know—

HOWARD: *When*?

JOHN: About a month ago.

HOWARD: *When* a month ago?

JOHN: The same day you stole those boots from my feet. That's really not fair, man—

HOWARD: When that day?

JOHN: In the morning.

HOWARD: What time?

JOHN: I don't have a watch.

HOWARD: Guess.

JOHN: Early.

HOWARD: Where did you see him?

JOHN: Here.

HOWARD: Under the pier?

JOHN: On the beach.

HOWARD: And?

JOHN: And what? That was the last time I saw him.

HOWARD: How did you end up with all his worldly goods?

JOHN: He gave them to me.

HOWARD: Why?

JOHN: Said he didn't want them.

HOWARD: Uh huh.

JOHN: Listen, I don't ask a lot of questions when someone wants to do a good deed. I just say "thank you", "much obliged", "god bless you", bow three or four times, curtsy, cry, tip my hat, and go on my merry way.

HOWARD: And where did he go?

JOHN: You're the detective.

HOWARD: Hey, you've already lied to me once. You better stop with the smart ass behavior and be straight with me. I'm getting paid to find this kid, and if you know something that will help, I suggest you start giving it up because you are already on your way to the police station as it is.

JOHN: Are you a police officer?

HOWARD: I was.

JOHN: But you're not now.

HOWARD: I'm a private investigator. But I still have friends—

JOHN: But you're not working for Los Angeles County. Or the state of California. You're just like a rent a cop or something—

HOWARD: Listen—

JOHN: Did they kick you out of the force?

HOWARD: No—

JOHN: You sleep with someone's wife—

HOWARD: No—

JOHN: Get drunk on the job—

HOWARD: No—

JOHN: Steal some drugs, shoot the wrong guy—

HOWARD: Listen, shithead. I retired. Respectfully—

JOHN: Have a mental break down. Lose your marbles—

HOWARD: No—

JOHN: Go berserk?

HOWARD: *Respectfully.* I wanted to make my own hours and be my own boss. Spend time with my family.

JOHN: So you had trouble with authority figures.

(Silence)

HOWARD: Let's not worry so much about my life. Alright?

JOHN: I've got nothing to hide.

HOWARD: Yeah.

JOHN: I've got no skeletons in my closet. Nope. I'm free. Not like you.

HOWARD: I don't know anyone on the streets without a skeleton.

JOHN: I'm a bum. Nothing more to it than that. I hate bosses and I hate working.

HOWARD: What happened to Boudin?

JOHN: And I don't care much for schedules.

HOWARD: What happened to Boudin?

JOHN: I guess my resume's nothing to cheer about either. Kinda slim on the references.

HOWARD: What happened to Boudin?

JOHN: I do not know.

HOWARD: That's not good enough.

JOHN: He left me his pack because he said he didn't need it anymore. When I asked him where he was going, and he wouldn't tell me. I left to hide it, for safe keeping, came back to the beach, his boots were here, and he was gone. End of story.

HOWARD: Uh huh.

JOHN: Put me under a lie detector and I'll prove it.

HOWARD: Really?

JOHN: As the ocean and sky are my witness.

(*Silence*)

HOWARD: You think he drowned himself?

JOHN: No.

HOWARD: Why not?

JOHN: I would have seen it.

HOWARD: You could have missed it.

JOHN: I see it all.

HOWARD: What, you God now?

JOHN: What if I was?

HOWARD: Shut up.

JOHN: Of course, I'd wear better shoes. And I might keep some angels around me. Those Victoria Secret angels. And I'd have a side-kick. Just a little guy, with a good sense of humor. You know, a guy who doesn't mind playing second fiddle, and thinks I'm smarter than he is.

HOWARD: Alright—

JOHN: I'd probably eat better too. Filet Mignon. Pizza. Carrots. I'd let my side-kick open the wine. Hey, you wanna be my side-kick?

(HOWARD *looks at* JOHN.)

JOHN: You're right. Your ego couldn't hack it.

HOWARD: Boudin could have gone toward the water—

JOHN: Nope. No. I tell you. I would have seen him. I walk this beach every morning. Nothing on the sand but cigarette butts, chicken bones, condoms, and plastic bags. You'd be surprised how much trash washes up. People are nasty—

HOWARD: Uh huh.

JOHN: But he was pretty shook up about something.

HOWARD: What?

JOHN: That I couldn't tell you.

HOWARD: How do you know he was shook up?

JOHN: I've seen shook up. I know what shook up looks like in a man.

HOWARD: What's it look like?

JOHN: Look at me.

HOWARD: We're not talking about you—

JOHN: I may have one skeleton, I guess. But only one.

HOWARD: We're not talking about you.

JOHN: Hell. Use your imagination.

HOWARD: I don't want to use my imagination.

JOHN: He was shook up about something. Upset. Crying and so forth. Shook up! You're the detective—

HOWARD: Something that might make him want to kill himself?

JOHN: I don't know!

HOWARD: Was he feeling helpless?

JOHN: Maybe.

HOWARD: Alone?

JOHN: Of course.

HOWARD: Well—

JOHN: But that doesn't make me want to kill myself.

HOWARD: We're not talking about you.

JOHN: That makes me want to run home to Mommy.

(JOHN *pulls the journal from his pocket, and tosses it to* HOWARD.)

(*Music*)

(Video: Santa Monica Pier: A father passes a baby off to his mother.)

Scene 5

(The Living Room)

HOWARD: Were you going to tell me?

(LIZA and WESLEY on the couch. HOWARD sits awkwardly between them, holding Emmett's journal. He's waiting for them to say something. Waiting)

WESLEY: I was.

HOWARD: When?

LIZA: Would anyone like a cup of coffee?

WESLEY: I wanted to tell you about that in the beginning. Right from the start—

LIZA: Or tea?

WESLEY: But Liza wouldn't let me.

LIZA: That's not true—

WESLEY: She was afraid you'd think we were bad people. Are we bad people, Liza?

LIZA: Can we please not chew at each other so? In front of—

WESLEY: Personally, I just want to get my son home so I can beat the shit out of him. Worry is time consuming. And I don't like to waste time. But when Liza found out my mother had money, and left it all to Emmett, she said we had a right to have some of it.

(LIZA pushes a smile.)

LIZA: I never said that. I never said that. Cocktail?

WESLEY: Boloney.

LIZA: Wesley—

WESLEY: My parents didn't give me a pot to piss in growing up. (They gave me a stick of gum, and seat in the back of the car with four other kids.) And since my father died, my mother barely left the house. How the hell did she get rich? Then we got a hold of her will. Turns out, years ago, unbeknownst to any us, she bought stock in one thing: Oil. And the entire inheritance, stuck in a bank in Los Angeles. All that money, was left to my one and only, holier than thou, lazy-ass son. Which will only give him more incentive to never settle down or be a responsible person or a decent citizen.

LIZA: Wesley—

WESLEY: He's lived off other people all his life, and now he's got a life-time ticket down easy street, and I got more worry. Well, Liza here didn't want to see that happen.

(LIZA *just stares straight ahead.*)

WESLEY: Right Liza?

LIZA: I really don't care about the money. I just want to see my son.

WESLEY: Liza.

LIZA: It's true.

WESLEY: You want a new house, with a new back yard, so you can have a lap pool. Don't go playing the concerned mother—

LIZA: I'm not playing anything, Wesley!

WESLEY: C'mon!

(LIZA *regains her cool.*)

LIZA: All I told you—I simply told him, that I thought that that was an awful lot of money for one person, and since we hadn't heard from Emmett in some time, we might want to see if we could find him and talk to him about what he had in mind to do with his inheritance.

WESLEY: "If he'd share it."

LIZA: We've always shared everything with him. It's not so much to ask. That's what family is for.

WESLEY: See?

LIZA: What?

WESLEY: A pit bull.

(WESLEY *smiles while* LIZA *straightens her skirt.*)

LIZA: I don't know what you're talking about.

(LIZA *pushes a smile.* HOWARD *looks at them both, gets up, taking the journal with him, and walks out—*)

LIZA: Coffee?

(*Video: Boots walking on pavement. [Run under next scene]*)

Scene 6

(ROOSTER *stands with his cell phone. The dog beside him*)

ROOSTER: He always called early in the morning...last time I didn't pick up...I just didn't feel like talking...he didn't say anything, but I knew it was him...there was nothing but silence and static for along time...then a weird awful sob...I still have the message. I can't seem to delete it...I don't know what he wanted...I didn't want to know...I just—if I had known that something was wrong, or that he was in trouble, that he might do something...that he really needed me...that I'd never see him again, I would have...I just...
(*He takes in the thought of Emmett being really Gone. Pushing tears*)
I would have picked up...I would have helped...

(*He wipes his eyes, embarrassed:*)

(The secret pact of crybabies.)

(He tries to get himself together.)

If you think I'm a bad best friend…well, truth is, we're not that close anymore…not since Sally and I— and I tried to apologize for that. I did…I don't know why we both wanted to hurt him, but we did…He just gets everything he wants. Everything… It's not fair…I'm just some guy he calls now…when he wants something…nine out of ten times he calls, he never asks one fucking question about me. Not one. What kind of friend is that?

Scene 7

(Living room)

(LIZA alone on the couch.)

LIZA: Of course it's not just about the money. What kind of mother would I be if I only cared about my son's inheritance? Please. Wesley exaggerates. Just like his mother. They blow everything way out of proportion and suddenly a whole three act drama is made from a silly pin drop or a quiet suggestion… Emmett is first and foremost, and always will be, my son. No amount of money could replace him. Not a penny. And Wesley knows that. For some reason I am always the bad guy in this house. Nothing I do has ever been…

(She straightens that skirt.)

All I said was that I think we need to talk to Emmett about this change, in his life. This big change. It can confuse a person… Two million dollars is a lot of money for a young man to find himself in charge of, and he's never been responsible about money. Never. He's so…Emmett is really very full of himself. Full of his big ideas and everything that Wesley and I did

at a certain point, in his opinion, were mindless and
"bourgeois". I couldn't put a meal on the table—I
couldn't express a word, without getting an eye roll,
a sigh, and a sermon from my son. "For Christ's sake,
Mom, casserole!"…"Wonder what sweatshop that shirt
came from, Dad." "Why don't you two just pack up
your spoon collection and your Prozac prescriptions
and move to Miami already. Your mind and your
marriage is dead. Why not let what's left of you die
with a tan." So on and so forth. Endless commentary
on everything little thing we said or did. But especially
me. I got it from my hair, right down to my slippers.
"Morning, Liberace." They're slippers! What does it
matter if they sparkle! …So, at first, honestly, I was
glad not to hear from him… Just to get a break from
his, his preaching…But then one year passed, then two,
two turned to four. Four years is almost forever. And
now he's got all that money? "Oil money", no less. I'm
afraid he's going to do something stupid with it. Like
burn it. Or give it away to a some charity no one has
heard of. Or run away even farther. And then no one in
the family will ever have a chance to see him again or
do anything about it. He'll be done with us, for good.
And then—

(WESLEY *comes and joins* LIZA. *She stops talking.*)

WESLEY: What?

(LIZA *smiles.*)

WESLEY: I lost something in the garage.

LIZA: What?

WESLEY: My mother.

LIZA: What do you mean?

WESLEY: Her ashes. They're not there.

LIZA: Don't be silly.

WESLEY: I'm not be silly, Liza. They're gone.

LIZA: I told you you shouldn't have left them there in the first place.

WESLEY: I didn't want them in the house.

LIZA: You have no sense of, of—

WESLEY: Of what?

LIZA: Propriety.

WESLEY: It's a box of ashes. Mom's not in there anymore—

LIZA: Still—

WESLEY: I wouldn't bring a pile of dog poop in the house just because I once loved the dog that left it behind—

LIZA: There's a big difference—

WESLEY: No there's not.

LIZA: Yes there is.

WESLEY: Well, what's it matter. The box is gone.

LIZA: Did you throw it out?

WESLEY: No.

LIZA: Are you sure?

WESLEY: Liza.

LIZA: What?

WESLEY: Don't insult me.

(Silence)

LIZA: Well. That's certainly odd.

WESLEY: We might have to hire Mr Howard to look for Emmett *and* my mother. Do a two-for-one.

LIZA: Please.

WESLEY: I hope a box of ashes is easier to find.

LIZA: Please.

WESLEY: Of course if the wind blows, it's a lost cause.

LIZA: Please.

WESLEY: Maybe so is Emmett.

LIZA: Wesley.

WESLEY: He could be, at this point.

LIZA: Don't say that.

WESLEY: Could be, Liza.

LIZA: Don't say it—

WESLEY: You haven't thought the same thing?

LIZA: No.
(Silence)
Besides, thinking it and saying it aloud…are two very different things.

WESLEY: How so?

LIZA: Saying it could make it true.

WESLEY: You're splitting hairs, honey.

(LIZA gets up.)

WESLEY: Where are you going?

LIZA: To see if I can find your mother. *(She exits.)*

(WESLEY sighs, lies down on the couch. Stares at the ceiling)

WESLEY: I really just wanted a quiet life. Security.
(Turns to look at the audience)
A good job, a good-looking wife who could cook, two well-behaved kids, a two-car garage, a chance to play golf every other Sunday. Grandkids to take fishing.
(He returns his attention to the ceiling.)
I guess the job turned out alright.

(Video: Skid Row, downtown L A. Dangerous even in the day time. Lost souls everywhere. [Runs behind the next 2 scenes])

(MIRANDA enters in night gown, pacing with the baby, humming him back to sleep, as:)

Scene 8

(SALLY plays with a silver chain around her neck.)

SALLY: He called late at night… He called when he was drunk…he told me he caught a ride with someone to California. (I always wanted to see Los Angeles. I guess he remembered that.) He told me he was going to eat oranges straight from the tree… He told me something was happening to him…something he couldn't explain…he kept me on the phone for hours, trying to explain, through mumbles and tears…while I kept him on the phone, begging him to just come home.

(WESLEY exits.)

(MIRANDA exits.)

(SALLY exits.)

Scene 9

HOWARD: Here's what we've got.

(HOWARD stands beside the U S map. Emmett's photo stuck in California with a pin. Surrounded by the pile of Emmett's things.)

HOWARD: This is what we've got.
(He looks over the stuff, picks up various things. [A coat. A sock. A blanket])
What's does this mean now? …Or this? Or this? What does any of it say about Emmett Boudin? That despite

himself, he accumulated just as much useless shit as
the rest of us? That despite himself, he is now, in some
form, defined by these objects? Understood by them?
Misunderstood?

(More stuff)

I mean look, he had taste. He bought the best sleeping
bag money could buy. High quality clothes. He bought
an expensive video camera. Shot all these pictures
of what? Why? (What are you trying to say, kid? It's
awful out there. Cruel. Unfair. Is that a surprise? I
could have told you that.)

(More stuff)

He was sentimental. Carried a picture of his son. He
was cautious. Kept a gun. He was critical. Punished
his parents for smothering him as a kid... Yet kept his
grandmother on a pedestal. So much so, that look, he
never sent any of the cards or letters he wrote to her.
Never sent a picture. Nothing. Why? Did he know that
a large inheritance was at stake? Did he really want the
money? (Did you want that money, kid? Did that make
you hate yourself? So what?! Grow up. You're not a
boy anymore. Men make sacrifices. Men make choices
they never thought they'd make. Men fail.)

*(By the end, he is throwing the things, searching. He stops,
picks up then smells one of the shirts.)*

Cigarettes. Sweat. Old Spice.

*(He puts on the shirt. He finds something in the pocket. He
pulls out his hand and it is covered in white ashes. He takes
a closer look.)*

Hello Grandma.

(He sighs, looks over at his map of the United States.)

What do you want, kid? You have everything you
need to do anything you want? Anything... All this
American possibility... Is this your true inheritance?
And ours?

(He looks over the stuff.)

Void?

Scene 10

(JOHN walks across the stage with Emmett's Nikon camera, the only thing he hid from HOWARD.)

(He snaps pictures left and right around him until he stops. He turns the camera towards himself and focuses on his own face...he smiles a big fake smile:)

JOHN: "Super-duper." *(And snaps the picture.)*

(He continues across the stage, taking pictures.)

Scene 11

(MIRANDA's living room.)

(HOWARD holds the baby, and sits with MIRANDA.)

HOWARD: I think he's asleep.

MIRANDA: Looks like it.

(Silence)

HOWARD: I should be going.

MIRANDA: Where to next?

HOWARD: *(Sighs)* Wherever the wind takes me, I guess. I might check out Alaska. Or the Carolinas. Maybe Mexico. Thank you for lunch.

MIRANDA: You're welcome.

HOWARD: You're a better cook than my wife. Of course, she's stopped cooking for me years ago.

MIRANDA: Nice of you to stop by.

HOWARD: All in a day's work. I have to stay in touch with people. Keep the lines of communication open.

MIRANDA: I'm sure he'll be home soon, Mr Howard.
And you can stop all this. Go home to your own
family. Get some sleep.

(HOWARD *carefully passes the baby off to* MIRANDA, *then
takes a letter out of his pocket.*)

HOWARD: I thought the kid might want this. I found it
in his father's stuff.

MIRANDA: Why would Joe want it?

(HOWARD *hands the letter to* MIRANDA.)

HOWARD: It's addressed to him.

(Silence)

MIRANDA: I wanted a child with Emmett's curiosity.
His thirst for the world. I don't have that. I'm practical.
I live in the same town I grew up in. I don't like
change. I pretty much accept status quo. I don't think
there's anything wrong with wanting that searching
quality in my son—

HOWARD: Of course not—

MIRANDA: Or wanting him to be as beautiful as his
father. And mine. I get to keep Joe—

HOWARD: Nothing wrong with that—

MIRANDA: I don't think so—

HOWARD: But he's not yours to keep. One day you
might get a brick through your heart because the world
has come to take him away. And then he's everybody's
son. Everybody's. But not yours.
(Silence)
Take care of yourself. And the kid.

MIRANDA: I, I will.

HOWARD: I mean, really keep an eye on him.
(He exits.)

(MIRANDA *sits down and opens the letter. She looks at the baby, and begins to read:*)

MIRANDA: "First of all, I'd like to say welcome. You weren't in any hurry to come into the world, and frankly, I can't blame you. It's a pretty confusing place. But you know, it's not all that bad either. You can do a lot of great things here. Like dancing. Dancing is good stuff. And driving. You can drive in a car for miles and miles with the music as loud as you want, and you can sing your heart out, and think you're a really good singer that no one's found out about yet. You can climb mountains and smell green (green has a smell) and feel fresh air in the early morning. Make a cup of coffee and drink it right then and man, that's living. You can swim in the ocean and taste the salt and feel sand on your skin and wonder what it's like to be a fish. You can have a dog. Dog's are the best; they'll lick your face and wag their tails every time they see you just because they're happy. They'll remind you to be happy about really simple things. Like dinner. You can meet lots of wonderful girls, and feel what it's like to kiss soft lips and smell sweet skin. You won't believe how good that will feel to you. I'm sorry, but words kinda fail in that area. Let's just say that it's a rush, of a million feelings you never knew you had until then. Of course, you may end up liking men, and you will feel the same things for them. Being loved by someone is probably the thing that makes coming into the world really worth the trip; worth the wild ride from Spiritland you just took to get here. (Hold on, buddy. It's just the beginning.) This is gonna sound like advice so please excuse me, but I've discovered, with a good love, all is well, Joe. You can feel at home in yourself then. I think that's all anyone's really looking for, to feel at home in their own body with someone who feels the same. I just want you to give that some thought.

And maybe learn how to do that with someone. Make
a home. Don't be a coward like your old man. Love.
Give yourself away to people with abandon. Don't give
pieces, give your whole self. And don't be afraid that
you're going to lose something, or fail. Just let them
have you, okay, Joe? That's courage. That's bravery,
son. The open heart. When I'm not here to watch
you grow up and help guide you through all these
wonderful and scary things you have ahead, you've
got to know, you've got to always remember, that I
love you. I do. You're going to doubt that down the
line, but I'm telling you now, I love you. Some people
believe that we pick our parents and you could be
picking me with the same criteria that I picked both my
parents, and I could be everything that you will strive
to avoid and I will respect you for that. More than you
know. Because while you picked a father that does
indeed love you and wish the best for you, he will not
stick around to raise you. Even if he feels it would be
the right thing to do. I'm just not the man for that, I'm
afraid. That's why you picked such a great Mom, you
see. She's going to raise you better than I ever could.
She's going to help you be a great man someday. And I
will be proud of you. I already am.".

Scene 12

(LIZA *stands in the corner of the stage, confiding. She wears
a nightgown.*)

LIZA: Months and months ago. Strangely enough, the
very night after we hired Mr Howard. I did think—I
thought I heard someone in the house. Footsteps in
Emmett's bedroom. I wasn't scared. I just thought,
Oh God, it could be him. We can call this whole
thing off…I was so excited. But I didn't dare wake
Wesley. Or turn on any lights. I learned long ago to

treat Emmett like a stray cat. If you get too close, he'll
run or he'll scratch you. You've got to be careful how
you approach him. So I just tip-toed down the hall
to his room, and stood there at the door, in the dark.
"Emmett baby, is that you? ...Emmett? Is that you? ...
We put your stuff in the garage, honey...don't worry,
it's there, if you want it...we kept it all...I promise."
No one answered. But Emmett has never answered
me when I talked to him directly. "I've missed you,
Emmett...I have...you will never know how very
much I've missed you."

(Video: A little boy walking on a sidewalk.)

*(*WESLEY *enters in his pajamas, creeping to the opposite
corner of the stage, holding the walkie-talkie to his ear,
waiting/listening...)*

LIZA: I didn't hear anything. Not even breathing.
It was just quiet and dark. "But Emmett?", I said,
"Guess what? You're rich, honey. Do you know that?.
Your grandmother's dead, sweetheart, I'm sorry, I
know you loved her very much...but it's all okay...
she took good care of you...you're set...you've got
the world at your feet...everything you'll ever need
and more...Emmett?" Still I didn't hear anything.
Finally, I couldn't help myself. I turned on the light.
His room was exactly the same as I left it. Nothing
in it but that treadmill I bought. But there, on top of
my new treadmill, was his wooden nickel. With the
face of a Cherokee Indian on it. Something he used to
carry in his pocket as a boy. His lucky nickel, he called
it. He kissed it when he wanted something special
to happen, when he was making a wish. (He had so
many wishes...the Cherokee's face was barely...) It
must have fallen out of his things when we carried
them away. So I picked it up and kissed it, and put
it back where I found it. Wesley was snoring when
I went back to bed. He never even heard a thing. I

suppose it was just the wind making that noise. Or my imagination. This old house makes lots of strange sounds at night. I was probably just hearing things I wanted to hear.

WESLEY: What's your 10/20, Emmett? ...Emmett? ... Emmett?

(Video: The little boy walks around a corner, out of frame, and disappears.)

(Black out)

END OF PLAY

www.ingramcontent.com/pod-product-compliance
Lightning Source LLC
Chambersburg PA
CBHW052216090426
42741CB00010B/2557